SECRET OF HEALING CONVERSATIONS

NURTURING PRINCIPLES IN COUNSELLING AND THERAPY

DR. MINAKSHI BANSAL

DEDICATION

This book is dedicated to all the therapists and counsellors whose unwavering dedication and compassion bring light into the darkest corners of the human experience. Your commitment to fostering growth and healing does not go unnoticed or unappreciated. May this work serve as a resource and inspiration, encouraging you to continue the vital work of nurturing and transforming lives.

ᑅᑅᑅ

Contents

Contents

Prayer

"Om Bhadram Karnebhih Shrinuyama Devah
Bhadram Pashyemakshabhiryajatrah
Sthirairangais Tushtuvamsastanubhih
Vyashema Devahitam Yadayuh
Svasti Na Indro Vriddhashravah
Svasti Nah Pusha Vishwavedah
Svasti Nastarkshyo Arishtanemih
Svasti No Brihaspatir Dadhatu
Om Shantih Shantih Shantih"

This mantra is a prayer for universal well-being, invoking the blessings of various deities for protection, health, and happiness. It emphasizes the importance of experiencing the auspicious through all senses and living a life aligned with divine purpose. The repetition of "Shantih" at the end signifies a deep desire for peace in the individual, the environment, and the universe at large. This mantra is often recited as a prayer for peace, prosperity, and the physical and spiritual well-being of all beings.

ɒɒɒ

About The Author

Dr. Minakshi Bansal, born in the bustling metropolis of Delhi, India, has led a life steeped in artistry, scholarly pursuit, and an unwavering commitment to societal betterment. Following her marriage, she relocated to Ahmedabad, Gujarat, where she has since blossomed into a multifaceted beacon of inspiration for many. Dr. Minakshi is not only recognized as a gifted artist in the realm of Fine Arts but also as an esteemed author, a devoted social worker and a dedicated research scholar in Psychology. Her journey, marked by a profound dedication to elevating those around her, especially the downtrodden and underprivileged children of society, is a testament to her deep-seated belief in the transformative power of engagement and empathy.

From her earliest days, Minakshi was distinguished by an insatiable appetite for reading. Her literary universe was inhabited by characters and narratives that spanned ethical tales, motivational and inspirational stories, and the mythic parables imbued with life lessons. This voracious reading habit was not merely for personal edification but was driven by a desire to distill and disseminate the essence of these narratives to foster the development of students and peers alike. She was particularly captivated by the lives and teachings of historical figures and spiritual leaders such as Adi Shankaracharya, Swami Vivekananda, Dr. APJ Abdul Kalam, Mahamana Pandit Madan Mohan Malviya, Mahatma Gandhi, Sardar Vallabhai Patel, and Vinoba Bhave, among others. Their philosophies and life stories fueled her ambition to embody their ideals of resilience, selflessness, and relentless pursuit of knowledge.

Dr. Minakshi's academic and practical engagement with psychology has been equally noteworthy. As a research scholar, her focus has been on exploring the intricate tapestry of the human psyche, aiming to unlock the potential for psychological well-being and societal harmony. Her scholarly work is complemented by her active involvement in social work, where she employs her academic insights to make tangible differences in the lives of the underprivileged. Her endeavours in social work are characterized by an innovative approach that combines traditional wisdom with contemporary psychological practices to address the multifaceted challenges faced by these communities.

Her artistic talents, another facet of her diverse capabilities, are not merely a personal passion but also serve as a medium through which she communicates and connects with others. Her art, rich in symbolism and emotional depth, reflects her philosophical inquiries and social concerns, offering viewers a glimpse into the breadth of her intellect and the depth of her compassion.

In addition to her contributions to the arts and social sciences, Dr. Minakshi has embraced the healing arts of Pranic Healing, mastering the techniques developed by Master Choa Kok Sui. This practice, which focuses on the manipulation of Prana or life energy to heal the body and aura, has been both a personal journey of discovery and a means through which she extends her healing touch to others. Her proficiency in Pranic Healing is complemented by her advocacy and teaching of various forms of meditation aimed at rejuvenation, personal betterment, and the cultivation of harmony within individuals and communities alike.

Dr. Minakshi's life is a narrative of relentless pursuit, not just of personal achievement but of the upliftment and empowerment of society at large. Her diverse interests and talents—spanning the arts, literature, psychology, and the healing practices—converge on a singular path of service. She embodies the spirit of the luminaries who inspired her, channelling their legacy through her actions and teachings. Through her books, art, and social initiatives, she continues to inspire a new generation to embark on their own journeys of self-discovery, resilience, and altruism.

Her commitment to social betterment, particularly her focus on uplifting underprivileged children, reflects a deep understanding of the transformative potential of education and personal development. By integrating her knowledge of psychology, her artistic sensibilities, and her healing practices, Dr. Bansal has developed a holistic approach to social work that addresses both the immediate needs and the long-term well-being of the communities she serves.

As an author, Dr. Minakshi's writings offer a blend of inspirational insights, practical wisdom, and reflective contemplations drawn from her extensive reading and life experiences. Her books serve as a guide for those seeking to navigate the complexities of life with grace, resilience, and purpose. Through her narratives, she extends an invitation to her readers to explore the depths of their own potential and to contribute meaningfully to the collective well-being of society.

In Dr. Minakshi Bansal, we find a remarkable synthesis of the artist, the scholar, the healer, and the social activist. Her life's work stands as a beacon of hope and a source of inspiration for individuals seeking to make a difference in the world. Her story is a compelling reminder of the power of individual action, rooted in compassion and driven by a profound commitment to the betterment of humanity. Dr. Minakshi's legacy is not just in the tangible outcomes of her efforts but in the enduring spirit of inquiry, empathy, and service that she embodies.

ppp

Preface

As we navigate the intricacies of human relationships and the complexities of individual psyches, the need for meaningful and transformative conversations in therapeutic settings becomes increasingly evident. The journey of creating this book stemmed from a deep-seated desire to distill the essence of what makes therapeutic interactions not just effective, but genuinely healing and transformative. It is an exploration aimed at both seasoned practitioners and aspiring counselors, as well as anyone interested in understanding the profound impact that thoughtful, empathetic communication can have on healing.

The art of fostering healing through conversation is both ancient and innately human; however, it is also a skill that requires refinement and understanding. In my years of practice, I have observed numerous interactions in various therapeutic contexts—each interaction providing a unique window into the human condition. These experiences have been instrumental in shaping the perspectives shared in this book. They have taught me that the true power of therapy lies not only in the methodologies employed but in the quality of the connection that develops through genuine, empathetic dialogue.

Throughout this work, I delve into the fundamental aspects of nurturing conversations that can facilitate profound change. From the subtle dynamics of body language to the explicit techniques of verbal exchange, every element of interaction plays a crucial role in the therapeutic process. The concepts discussed are grounded in contemporary psychological research, yet they are also imbued with the timeless wisdom of therapeutic traditions that span cultures and epochs.

This book is structured to guide you through various principles of effective therapeutic communication, each chapter building upon the last to weave a comprehensive tapestry of strategies and insights. It begins with the core skills of active listening and empathy, which form the foundation of all healing interactions. From there, it explores more nuanced topics such as the management of transference and countertransference, the strategic use of questions, and the delicate balance of giving feedback that can empower without overwhelming.

A significant portion of the text is devoted to the practical application of these skills in real-world therapeutic scenarios. These include detailed discussions on navigating the complexities of individual differences, cultural sensitivities, and the inevitable challenges that arise in any therapeutic relationship. The aim is to equip therapists with the tools necessary not only to respond to a wide range of clinical situations but also to foster an environment where clients feel truly seen, heard, and understood.

Moreover, this book addresses the personal development of therapists themselves. It underscores the importance of self-reflection, continuous learning, and the critical need for self-care. Being a therapist is not merely about administering techniques; it is about being present, human, and empathetic, which requires one to be in tune with one's own emotional and psychological well-being.

The process of writing this book has been a journey of reflection and synthesis, striving to encapsulate the subtle art of therapeutic conversation in a manner that is both informative and accessible. My hope is that it serves as a valuable resource for enhancing the practice of therapists at all stages of their careers. Whether you are a student just beginning to explore the field of psychology or a seasoned practitioner seeking to deepen your understanding of therapeutic communication, the insights within these pages are intended to inspire and guide you.

As you turn these pages, I invite you to engage with the material not just intellectually, but with your whole being. The secrets to healing conversations are not just in the techniques and theories but in the space between words, where connection and transformation occur. Let this book be a companion on your journey toward mastering the art of these conversations, enhancing your role not just as a therapist but as a facilitator of true healing.

In closing, I extend my deepest gratitude to you, the reader, for joining me in exploring the profound dimensions of therapeutic dialogue. It is my sincere wish that the contents of this book enrich your practice and the lives of those you touch through your professional journey. Here's to the conversations that heal, the words that empower, and the silence that speaks volumes.

Dr. Minakshi Bansal
Social Activist
Ahmedabad, Gujarat, Bharat

ϷϷϷ

ONE

THE ART OF ACTIVE LISTENING: BEYOND HEARING WORDS

Active listening is the cornerstone of effective therapy and counselling. It involves much more than merely hearing the words spoken by clients. At its heart, active listening requires a deep level of engagement, where the therapist not only hears the words but also fully comprehends, acknowledges, and responds appropriately to communicate that understanding back to the client.

The essence of active listening is attentiveness. Therapists must cultivate the ability to focus entirely on the client, setting aside their own thoughts and distractions. This involves observing not just what is being said, but how it is said—the tone, pace, and volume of speech, as well as non-verbal cues like facial expressions and body language. Such attentiveness helps the therapist to capture the emotional undertones of the client's words, which are often as important as the words themselves.

Empathy plays a critical role in active listening. It allows therapists to put themselves in their clients' shoes, seeing the world from their perspective. This empathetic engagement is not about sympathy, which is feeling for the client, but rather feeling with the client, which fosters a deeper connection and understanding. When clients feel understood, they are more likely to open up and share deeper thoughts and feelings, which are crucial for effective therapy.

The process of active listening also involves reflecting and paraphrasing. By feeding the client's words back to them in a new way, therapists help clarify the thoughts and feelings expressed, ensuring that both therapist and client are on the same page. This can also help clients see their thoughts from a new perspective, which can be very enlightening and often therapeutic in itself.

Questioning is another vital aspect of active listening. Therapists use open-ended questions that encourage detailed responses rather than simple yes or no answers. Such questions help probe deeper into the client's issues without leading them to a predetermined conclusion. This technique helps in uncovering underlying issues that might not be apparent, even to the client, at the beginning of the session.

Active listening is a dynamic process. It requires the therapist to be both a speaker and a listener, engaging in a dance of verbal and non-verbal exchanges. This dynamic process allows the therapy session to evolve naturally, with the therapist gently guiding the conversation to help the client explore their thoughts and feelings in a structured yet open-ended manner.

Building trust is an essential outcome of effective active listening. When clients feel heard and understood, they develop trust in the therapeutic relationship. Trust is crucial for effective therapy as it creates a safe space where clients feel comfortable sharing sensitive or painful information. The security of this environment allows clients to explore their emotions and experiences more fully, which is critical for healing and growth.

Active listening is an art that goes beyond simple auditory skills. It involves a holistic approach to communication, requiring therapists to use a combination of emotional intelligence, empathy, and conversational skills to engage clients in a meaningful and therapeutic dialogue. Through active listening, therapists can create a supportive and understanding environment that facilitates healing and personal growth for their clients. This foundational skill sets the stage for all other aspects of therapy, making it a critical first step in any therapeutic relationship.

ᕼᕼᕼ

"Active listening goes beyond hearing words; it's about understanding the emotions and stories woven between them. When we truly listen, we open doors to healing that were once hidden behind silent walls."

ᗡᗡᗡ

TWO

CREATING SAFE SPACES: THE FOUNDATION OF TRUST

Creating safe spaces in therapy and counseling is integral to fostering trust, which is a foundational element of any therapeutic relationship. A safe space is characterized not just by physical safety, but emotional and psychological safety as well. This kind of environment allows clients to open up about their deepest fears, challenges, and uncertainties without fear of judgment, ridicule, or breach of confidentiality.

To begin with, the physical environment of therapy sessions plays a crucial role in establishing a safe space. The setting should be comfortable and private, ensuring that the client feels secure and undisturbed during sessions. Factors such as lighting, seating arrangement, and overall ambiance should be considered carefully to enhance comfort and facilitate a sense of calm and safety. For instance, soft, warm lighting and quiet, private spaces can help in reducing anxiety and making the client feel more at ease.

However, the true essence of creating safe spaces lies in the emotional and psychological aspects. Therapists must establish clear boundaries from the outset, which includes explaining the limits of confidentiality, session protocols, and mutual respect for personal boundaries. This clarity helps clients understand the framework within which they can safely express themselves.

Moreover, the therapist's demeanor plays a critical role. Therapists should exhibit qualities such as empathy, warmth, and non-judgmental understanding. The way therapists react to sensitive disclosures impacts the client's sense of safety dramatically. By responding with empathy and without judgment, therapists reinforce the safety of the therapeutic environment. Clients need to feel that their emotional experiences are valid and that they are in a space where their feelings and thoughts are taken seriously.

Building trust is a gradual process that evolves as the therapist consistently demonstrates understanding, respect, and confidentiality. Trust is crucial because it underpins the client's willingness to share more personal thoughts and feelings, which are essential for effective therapy. When clients trust their therapists, they are more likely to engage deeply in the therapeutic process, which can lead to more significant outcomes.

Effective communication is another vital component of creating safe spaces. Therapists must be skilled in both verbal and non-verbal communication. Active listening, as previously discussed, is part of this, but so is the way therapists convey understanding and empathy through their tone of voice, facial expressions, and body language. The therapist's ability to communicate effectively can help reinforce a client's feeling of being understood and supported.

Furthermore, therapists should be aware of and sensitive to issues of diversity, including cultural, sexual, and religious backgrounds.

Recognizing and honoring these aspects of a client's identity is part of creating a safe, respectful, and inclusive space. It requires therapists to be educated and aware of different cultural norms and values and to incorporate this understanding into their practice.

The creation of safe spaces in therapy is multi-faceted, involving the physical setting, the therapist's behavior, effective communication, and a deep respect for privacy and diversity. These elements come together to build a foundation of trust that allows clients to explore their issues in depth, engage in meaningful self-reflection, and ultimately achieve personal growth and healing. This foundational trust is not just beneficial for the therapeutic process but is also essential for the client's overall experience and satisfaction with therapy.

ᗒᗒᗒ

"Empathy is the heart's way of touching another
soul. In therapy, it's not just about understanding
what you are told, it's about feeling it too. This
connection is where healing begins."

ᗡᗡᗡ

THREE

EMPATHY IN ACTION: CONNECTING WITH EMOTIONS

Empathy is at the core of all effective counseling and therapy. It is the therapeutic tool that allows practitioners to connect with their clients on a deep emotional level, facilitating understanding and support that transcends mere verbal communication. Empathy involves not only understanding clients' emotions and experiences from their perspective but also communicating this understanding back to them, validating their feelings and promoting healing.

The first step in demonstrating empathy is active listening, which has been discussed as a fundamental skill in therapy. However, empathy extends beyond listening to include the therapist's responses and their ability to connect with the client's emotional state. This connection is crucial because it helps clients feel seen and understood, which can be profoundly therapeutic in itself.

Empathetic engagement involves more than just understanding the emotions as they are expressed; it requires a sensitivity to pick up on what is unspoken—subtle cues in body language, tone of voice, and facial expressions. Therapists must be attuned to these non-verbal signals to fully grasp the emotions and experiences that might not be directly communicated. This deep level of understanding helps therapists to provide responses that resonate with the client's emotional state, fostering a stronger therapeutic alliance.

One of the powerful aspects of empathy in action is its role in validating the client's feelings. Validation does not mean agreeing with the client's perceptions or feelings; rather, it acknowledges their emotions as real and significant. This acknowledgment is crucial for clients, particularly those who may have been marginalized or whose feelings have been dismissed in other areas of their lives. By affirmatively recognizing the client's emotional experience, therapists can enhance clients' self-esteem and encourage them to explore these feelings more deeply.

Empathy also involves a delicate balance of proximity and distance—being close enough to understand the client's feelings while maintaining a professional distance that allows for effective and objective therapy. This balancing act is crucial in maintaining the boundaries of the therapeutic relationship, ensuring that the therapist does not become so emotionally involved that it interferes with the client's path to self-discovery and healing.

Furthermore, the expression of empathy must be genuine. Clients are often highly sensitive to perfunctory displays of concern, which can be counterproductive. Genuine empathy requires therapists to be sincerely engaged and interested in the well-being of their clients, which builds trust and encourages openness. This authenticity in the therapist's demeanor reassures clients that their feelings are taken seriously and that the therapeutic space is a safe environment for emotional exploration.

Empathy also plays a critical role in handling difficult or intense emotional situations within therapy sessions. When clients express strong emotions, the empathetic response of the therapist can help to soothe and calm them, providing a sense of security and understanding. This supportive presence enables clients to work through intense emotions safely and constructively, which is often necessary for healing and personal growth.

Empathy is not only beneficial for clients but also enriches the therapeutic process. It allows therapists to gain deeper insights into the psychological and emotional dynamics of their clients, which can guide the therapeutic approach and interventions. Moreover, the empathetic connection can be a healing experience for clients, as it provides a model of compassionate, attentive, and respectful interaction that they can take into their daily lives.

Empathy is a vital component of successful therapy. It enhances the therapeutic relationship by creating a bond of trust and understanding, allows for deeper exploration of emotional issues, and provides the support clients need to embark on the journey of self-discovery and healing. Through empathy, therapists not only understand their clients' emotions but also foster an environment conducive to growth and change.

"Creating a safe space in therapy is like building a
sanctuary where fears and hopes can coexist. It is
here that vulnerability turns into strength, and
silence speaks louder than words."

❥❥❥

FOUR
THE POWER OF VALIDATION: AFFIRMING EXPERIENCES

Validation in the context of therapy and counseling is a crucial technique that helps clients feel acknowledged and accepted. It involves recognizing and accepting a client's feelings, thoughts, and experiences as valid and understandable within their personal context. This practice is not about agreeing with the client or condoning their behavior, but rather about acknowledging their feelings and experiences as real and significant. The act of validating is profoundly impactful as it can help build self-esteem, ease anxiety, and promote deeper and more honest communication.

The importance of validation stems from its ability to confirm that a person's experiences are legitimate. For many clients, just the feeling that their internal experiences are acknowledged can be therapeutic. This is especially true for individuals who have been marginalized or misunderstood by their families, communities, or societal structures. In such cases, validation acts as a corrective emotional experience—it counters the effects of having their feelings and perceptions consistently devalued or ignored.

Validation within therapy can take several forms, but all aim to convey empathy, support, and understanding. It often involves verbal expressions by the therapist that resonate with the client's emotional state. Phrases like "It makes sense that you feel..." or "Your reaction is completely understandable given the situation," help clients see that their emotional responses are normal or expected under the circumstances. This kind of feedback can relieve feelings of isolation and abnormality, reinforcing the client's sense of self and reducing internal conflict.

Beyond verbal affirmation, validation also involves non-verbal cues such as nodding, maintaining eye contact, and adopting an open body posture. These non-verbal behaviors communicate attentiveness and respect, further enhancing the client's sense of being valued and understood. It is crucial that both verbal and non-verbal validations are genuinely conveyed; clients are usually highly perceptive of disingenuous gestures, which can undermine the therapeutic relationship.

One of the therapeutic benefits of validation is its effect on the client's relationship with their emotions. Many individuals arrive at therapy with a history of suppressing or criticizing their emotional responses. Through validation, therapists can encourage clients to accept and explore their feelings rather than dismiss or fight against them. This acceptance is pivotal in emotional regulation and can lead to more adaptive coping strategies. Clients learn to approach their emotions with curiosity and compassion, which are vital steps in the healing process.

Moreover, validation plays a significant role in building and maintaining trust between the client and therapist. When clients feel that their personal experiences are validated, they are more likely to open up and share more deeply, which enriches the therapeutic dialogue. A strong, trusting therapeutic relationship is essential for effective therapy, as it enables clients to engage with more challenging aspects of their experiences and consider new perspectives offered by the therapist.

The process of validating is not without its challenges. Therapists must balance validation with the need to challenge and encourage growth. Over-validation, especially of maladaptive behaviors or distorted perceptions, can be counterproductive. Therefore, therapists need to use their clinical judgment to determine when and how to validate effectively. This involves a nuanced understanding of the client's needs and the dynamics of each particular situation.

Furthermore, the skillful use of validation requires therapists to be highly attuned to the client's verbal and non-verbal expressions and to understand the context in which these expressions occur. This sensitivity enables therapists to discern the underlying emotions and conflicts that may need addressing. The ability to validate these underlying, often unarticulated, aspects of the client's experience can lead to breakthroughs in therapy.

Validation is a powerful therapeutic tool that affirms clients' feelings and experiences, fosters a positive therapeutic relationship, and promotes emotional healing and personal growth. By making clients feel understood and accepted, therapists can help them navigate their emotional landscapes more effectively, encouraging a healthier, more reflective relationship with themselves and with others.

❧❧❧

"Validation in therapy does not mean agreement,
but acknowledgment. It's seeing the world through
another's eyes and saying, 'Your view matters.' This
is how trust is built and healing is nurtured."

♥♥♥

FIVE

QUESTIONING WITH CARE: TECHNIQUES FOR DEEPER INSIGHT

Questioning is a fundamental skill in therapy, serving as a tool to delve deeper into a client's thoughts and emotions, uncover underlying issues, and facilitate self-discovery and healing. Effective questioning in a therapeutic context is markedly different from everyday questioning; it is carefully crafted, empathetic, and strategically used to encourage clients to reflect, clarify their thoughts, and explore their feelings more deeply.

The art of questioning begins with the type of questions asked. Open-ended questions are pivotal in therapy because they encourage a detailed response, giving clients the freedom to express themselves fully and explore their thoughts and feelings without restriction. Questions like "What was going through your mind at that moment?" or "How did that experience make you feel?" prompt clients to think deeply and provide insights that might not emerge through yes/no questions. These open-ended questions are essential for gaining a deeper understanding of the client's perspective and encouraging a richer dialogue.

Effective questioning also involves timing and pacing. Therapists must be attuned to the client's emotional state and the flow of the conversation to introduce questions at the appropriate moment. Asking questions too quickly can overwhelm clients or disrupt their thought process, whereas timing a question appropriately can lead to significant insights and progress in therapy. Therapists need to be patient, allowing clients time to reflect and respond on their own terms. This respectful pacing honors the client's need to process and articulate their thoughts and emotions in a supportive environment.

The tone and formulation of questions are also crucial. Questions should be posed in a way that is non-judgmental and open, avoiding any implication of criticism or leading the client towards a specific answer. This approach helps maintain a safe and trusting therapeutic environment where clients feel respected and free to express their true selves. The therapist's tone should convey genuine curiosity and empathy, reinforcing their commitment to understanding the client's experience from the client's own perspective.

Another technique in questioning is the use of reflective questions, which mirror back to the client what they have just expressed, but rephrased to encourage deeper exploration or clarification. For instance, if a client says, "I always feel left out at work," the therapist might respond with, "What makes you feel left out?" This type of questioning can help clients examine the specifics of their experiences and the emotions attached to them, promoting greater self-awareness and insight.

Therapists may also use exploratory questions to help clients consider different perspectives or explore potential contradictions in their thoughts and feelings. Questions like, "What might be another way of looking at this situation?" or "How do you think other people might view this?" challenge clients to think outside their habitual patterns and consider alternative interpretations or solutions. This broadening of perspective can be particularly helpful in tackling rigid thought patterns and behaviors that are common in many psychological issues.

Furthermore, therapists often employ motivational questions to encourage clients to think about changes they might wish to make or goals they might want to achieve. Questions such as, "What would you like to be different?" or "What steps could you take to start making a change?" can motivate clients to think about the future and consider what actions they might take to improve their situations. These questions help bridge the gap between current challenges and future possibilities, fostering a sense of hope and direction.

Questioning with care is a sophisticated skill that requires sensitivity, patience, and precision. By asking the right questions at the right time and in the right way, therapists can unlock deeper insights, facilitate effective communication, and ultimately support the client's journey towards healing and growth. This methodical yet flexible approach to questioning is vital for developing a deeper understanding of the client, strengthening the therapeutic alliance, and promoting meaningful changes within the therapeutic process.

 PPP

"The right question at the right time can be a key turning a lock inside a troubled mind. Questions in therapy are not just about seeking answers but about unlocking the truths buried deep within."

ᗡᗡᗡ

SIX

THE ROLE OF BODY LANGUAGE: SILENT SIGNALS IN THERAPY

Body language plays a critical role in the therapeutic setting, serving as a non-verbal form of communication that can reveal underlying emotions and attitudes that may not be expressed verbally. Understanding and interpreting body language is essential for therapists, as it provides additional insight into the client's feelings and can significantly enhance the effectiveness of the therapeutic process.

In therapy, body language encompasses a range of behaviors including facial expressions, posture, gestures, and even the physical distance between the therapist and the client. Each of these elements can communicate a wealth of information and either reinforce or contradict what is being said verbally. For therapists, being attuned to these silent signals can aid in understanding the client's emotional state and can guide the direction of the therapeutic conversation.

Facial expressions are perhaps the most immediate and expressive aspects of body language. They can convey emotions more rapidly and authentically than words, which may be filtered through social or personal censorship. A therapist's ability to read facial cues—like the furrowing of a brow, a fleeting look of sadness, or a quick smile—can provide important clues to feelings the client may not be ready or able to verbalize. For example, if a client discusses a seemingly positive experience but shows signs of distress through their facial expressions, it might prompt the therapist to explore underlying feelings or thoughts that the client might not be consciously aware of.

Similarly, posture and gesture are also telling components of body language in therapy. Open postures, where the arms are relaxed or slightly apart, can suggest that a client is open to discussion and comfortable in the therapeutic environment. In contrast, crossed arms or legs might indicate that a client is feeling defensive or closed off. Such cues can help therapists gauge a client's receptiveness to certain topics or therapeutic interventions and adjust their approach accordingly.

The physical arrangement of the therapy room can also influence the communication of body language. The distance between the therapist and the client, the seating arrangement, and even the presence or absence of physical barriers like desks can affect how open and safe a client feels. Therapists often use these arrangements intentionally to create a welcoming and non-threatening environment that encourages open dialogue and trust.

Therapists not only need to be skilled in interpreting their clients' body language but also in managing their own. The therapist's body language can greatly affect the therapeutic relationship and the client's comfort level. For instance, leaning slightly forward can be perceived as a sign of interest and engagement, while maintaining eye contact can communicate attentiveness and respect. Conversely, frequent checking of the clock or fidgeting can send a message of disinterest or impatience, which can hinder the development of trust and openness in the session.

Moreover, synchrony in body language between the therapist and client—often referred to as mirroring—can strengthen the therapeutic alliance. When a therapist subtly mirrors a client's posture or gestures, it can create a sense of rapport and empathy, making the client feel more understood and connected. However, this must be done with sensitivity and authenticity, as overt or inappropriate mirroring can be perceived as mimicking or mocking.

Therapists also use their knowledge of body language to help clients become more aware of their own non-verbal signals. This awareness can be therapeutic in itself, as clients learn to recognize and understand their own emotions better through the physical expressions that accompany them. This self-awareness can be particularly beneficial for clients who struggle with emotional expression, as it provides another avenue for understanding and articulating their internal experiences.

Body language is a vital component of communication in therapy. It offers both the therapist and the client a deeper, often unspoken level of understanding that can enrich the therapeutic dialogue. By effectively interpreting and utilizing body language, therapists can enhance their empathetic connection with clients, foster a more open and trusting therapeutic environment, and facilitate deeper insights and more meaningful progress in therapy.

ᗡᗡᗡ

"Handling transference is a dance between what is said and what is meant. It's about seeing not just the person in front of you, but the shadows of others they bring along. In understanding these shadows, we light the way for healing."

SEVEN

BOUNDARY SETTING: PROTECTING SPACE AND ENERGY

Boundary setting is an essential aspect of therapy that protects both the therapist and the client, ensuring that the therapeutic relationship remains professional, respectful, and effective. Proper boundaries help define the expectations and limits of the relationship, creating a safe environment that promotes healing and personal growth. Setting and maintaining these boundaries is crucial for managing the therapeutic space and energy, preventing issues like dependency, burnout, and ethical violations.

Boundaries in therapy cover a wide range of interactions and behaviors, from maintaining confidentiality and determining the length and frequency of sessions to more nuanced emotional and personal limits. Clear boundaries help clients understand the professional nature of the relationship, reinforcing that the therapeutic environment is a place of support, not a personal or social relationship. For therapists, boundaries are vital for self-care and effectiveness; they prevent over-involvement in clients' problems, which can compromise objectivity and emotional resilience.

One of the primary boundaries involves time. Session times should be clearly defined and adhered to by both therapist and client. This structure helps clients understand the professional framework of the therapy and respects both parties' time and commitments. It also prevents sessions from becoming overly lengthy, which can be emotionally draining and counterproductive. Similarly, boundaries around communication outside of sessions should be established, such as rules regarding email or phone contact, to ensure that the therapist's personal time is respected and that the client does not become overly reliant on the therapist for support.

Physical boundaries are also important in therapy. These can include decisions about the physical layout of the therapy room, such as seating arrangements that provide comfortable personal space. Physical touch, although sometimes therapeutic, must be used cautiously and always with the client's consent, keeping in mind the potential for misinterpretation and the importance of the client's autonomy and comfort.

Emotional boundaries are equally critical. Therapists must be careful not to become emotionally over-involved with clients. While empathy and compassion are key components of therapeutic work, therapists must maintain a professional detachment to stay objective and effective. This boundary helps protect therapists from burnout and compassion fatigue, which can occur if too much emotional energy is invested in clients' issues. It also protects clients from becoming emotionally dependent on their therapist, encouraging them to develop their own coping skills and resilience.

Another significant aspect of boundary setting is managing dual relationships, which occur when the therapist and client have a relationship outside of therapy, whether social, business, or otherwise. These relationships can create conflicts of interest and blur the lines of professional boundaries, potentially harming the client and the therapeutic process. Ethical guidelines generally discourage such dual relationships, and therapists must strive to avoid them or manage them with strict professional boundaries and transparency if unavoidable.

Therapists should also be clear about the limits of confidentiality, which is itself a boundary that protects the client's privacy. Clients should understand what confidentiality entails and its limits, such as the legal obligations therapists have to breach confidentiality in cases of threatened harm to self or others. Understanding these limits helps clients feel safe to share personal information, knowing it will be protected unless their safety or someone else's is at risk.

Setting and maintaining boundaries in therapy is a complex but essential task. It requires constant vigilance, clear communication, and mutual respect. Proper boundaries not only safeguard the therapeutic process but also enhance it by creating a structured, safe space where clients can explore their deepest issues without fear of judgment or breach of trust. For therapists, boundaries are a tool for self-care and professionalism, enabling them to provide the best possible support to their clients while maintaining their own well-being.

ppp

"Humor in therapy is like a ray of sunshine on a
cloudy day; it doesn't clear the sky but brightens the
path. It reminds us that even in the midst of
healing, there is room for laughter."

ᐁᐁᐁ

EIGHT

NAVIGATING RESISTANCE: TECHNIQUES FOR ENGAGEMENT

Resistance in therapy is a common challenge that reflects a client's reluctance or inability to engage fully with the therapeutic process. It can manifest in various forms, such as missed appointments, silence during sessions, minimal emotional expression, or even overt disagreement with the therapist's suggestions. Understanding and effectively navigating resistance is crucial for therapists, as it often signifies deeper issues that require attention and understanding.

Recognizing the Signs of Resistance

Resistance is not merely a barrier to therapy; it is often a communication about the client's feelings, fears, or unmet needs. It may indicate anxiety about the therapeutic process, fear of vulnerability, or discomfort with the emotions that therapy is bringing to the surface. Clients might also resist therapy if they feel misunderstood, judged, or pushed in a direction they are not ready to explore. Therefore, the first step in navigating resistance is recognizing it as a significant part of the client's response to therapy.

Strategies for Engaging Resistant Clients

Once resistance is identified, therapists can use several strategies to engage clients and encourage a more productive therapeutic interaction. These techniques focus on building trust, creating a safe environment, and aligning the therapy more closely with the client's needs and pace.

1. Creating a Safe Therapeutic Environment

A fundamental approach to mitigating resistance is to ensure that the therapy setting is perceived as a safe and supportive environment. This involves reinforcing the confidentiality of the sessions, demonstrating consistent respect for the client's views, and emphasizing the non-judgmental nature of therapy. Safety in the therapeutic context encourages clients to lower their defenses and engage more openly in the process.

2. Validating the Client's Feelings

Validation is a powerful tool in managing resistance. By acknowledging and affirming the client's feelings and perspectives, therapists can reduce the threat associated with vulnerability. Validation does not mean agreeing with all the client says but rather acknowledging that their feelings and reactions are understandable and legitimate. This acceptance can help break down resistance by aligning the therapist and client against the problem, not each other.

3. Adjusting the Pace of Therapy

Resistance can often be a sign that the therapy is moving too quickly or in a direction that feels uncomfortable for the client. In such cases, it is crucial for therapists to be flexible and adjust the pace of therapy to match the client's readiness to engage. Slowing down the process and allowing more time for the client to acclimate to the therapy can reduce resistance and facilitate a deeper exploration of challenging issues.

4. Using Reflective Listening

Reflective listening is an approach that involves mirroring back to the client what they have said, demonstrating that the therapist has accurately heard and understood their perspective. This technique can be particularly effective in reducing resistance, as it reassures the client that their voice is heard and valued in the therapeutic relationship.

5. Exploring the Resistance

Directly addressing the resistance can also be a strategy. By inviting the client to discuss their feelings about the therapy or their reluctance to engage with certain topics, therapists can uncover underlying concerns that may be driving the resistance. This exploration should be approached with sensitivity and curiosity, avoiding any implication that the client's resistance is problematic or unreasonable.

6. Incorporating Motivational Interviewing

Motivational interviewing is a client-centered approach designed to enhance motivation by helping clients explore and resolve ambivalence. This technique involves open-ended questions, affirmations, reflective listening, and summarizing to help clients articulate their motivations for change and the barriers they perceive. Motivational interviewing can be particularly effective for clients who are ambivalent about their capacity to change or the benefits of therapy.

7. Leveraging Therapeutic Alliances

Building a strong therapeutic alliance is perhaps the most critical factor in overcoming resistance. This alliance is based on trust, respect, and collaboration. When clients feel genuinely cared for and understood by their therapist, they are more likely to engage in the work necessary to change.

Navigating resistance requires a nuanced understanding of the client's experiences and needs. By employing strategies that emphasize safety, validation, careful pacing, and therapeutic alliance, therapists can effectively engage clients, transforming resistance into a pathway for deeper insight and lasting change. This approach not only facilitates progress in therapy but also empowers clients, enhancing their agency and commitment to their healing journey.

ᐅᐅᐅ

"Cultural sensitivity in therapy is essential; it's about seeing the person, not just the problem. By honoring where a person comes from, we guide them more effectively to where they need to go."

❧❧❧

NINE

CULTIVATING PATIENCE: THE PACE OF PROGRESS

In therapy, progress can often be slow and non-linear, challenging both the client's and the therapist's expectations of change. Cultivating patience is essential in the therapeutic process, as it acknowledges the complexities of human behavior and emotional healing. Patience in therapy is about more than merely waiting; it is an active, intentional practice that fosters a supportive environment conducive to gradual change and self-discovery.

Understanding the Nature of Therapeutic Change

Therapeutic change involves altering deeply ingrained behaviors, thought patterns, and emotional responses, which is inherently a complex and gradual process. Each client's journey is unique, influenced by their personal history, resilience, support systems, and the specific challenges they face. Therapists must recognize the individual nature of each client's healing process and set realistic expectations for the pace of change. This understanding is crucial in cultivating patience and maintaining a supportive, non-pressurized therapeutic environment.

The Role of Therapist Patience

Therapist patience is fundamental in modeling a calm, accepting presence that reassures clients they are in a safe space where they can explore their thoughts and feelings without haste. When therapists convey patience, both through their demeanor and verbal expressions, it helps clients feel valued and understood, regardless of how slow their progress might seem. This validation is crucial for clients who may be struggling with self-criticism or discouragement about their perceived lack of progress.

Additionally, therapist patience helps in building and sustaining a strong therapeutic alliance. When clients see that their therapist is willing to stay with them through slow and challenging periods without judgment, their trust in the therapeutic process strengthens. This trust is a key factor in effective therapy, as it encourages clients to take greater risks in exploring difficult topics and making meaningful changes.

Facilitating Client Patience

Part of a therapist's role is to help clients cultivate patience with themselves. This involves teaching clients to recognize and celebrate small achievements and to understand that setbacks are a normal part of the healing journey. Therapists can facilitate this understanding through techniques such as mindfulness, which encourages clients to stay present-focused and appreciate incremental progress. Regular reflections on the therapy process can also help clients see how they have evolved, reinforcing the value of patience and persistence.

Strategies for Cultivating Patience in Therapy

Setting Clear, Achievable Goals: Breaking down larger therapeutic goals into smaller, manageable objectives can help make the process feel more attainable and less overwhelming. This approach not only makes progress more visible but also provides regular opportunities for positive reinforcement, which can motivate both client and therapist.

Educating Clients About the Therapy Process: Clients often come into therapy with little understanding of how it works and what to expect. Educating them about the nature of emotional healing, the reasons for the methods used, and the typical challenges encountered during therapy can help set realistic expectations and foster patience.

Encouraging Self-Compassion: Cultivating self-compassion is a powerful way for clients to develop patience with themselves. This involves learning to treat oneself with the same kindness, concern, and support that one would show to a good friend. Therapists can teach self-compassion practices that help clients tolerate discomfort and frustration, which are often parts of the therapeutic process.

Using Mindfulness Techniques: Mindfulness helps clients and therapists alike stay grounded in the present moment, fostering a patient attitude towards the therapy process. Techniques such as breathing exercises, guided imagery, or mindful observation can help clients manage anxiety about the future and impatience with the pace of their progress.

Reflecting on Past Successes: Regularly reflecting on the moments of progress and breakthrough in therapy can reinforce the value of patience. These reflections can be integrated into therapy sessions to remind clients that growth is often subtle and cumulative.

Cultivating patience is a vital aspect of effective therapy. It involves understanding and accepting the slow and complex nature of personal change, supporting clients in their unique journeys, and maintaining a therapeutic environment that honors the time it takes to achieve lasting transformation. Patience, cultivated by both therapist and client, becomes not just a strategy for managing the therapeutic process but a transformative quality that can lead to deeper self-awareness, resilience, and ultimately, healing.

ᐁᐁᐁ

"Ethical practice in therapy is the backbone of trust.
It requires more than following rules; it demands a
commitment to respect the humanity of the person
seeking help. This commitment is the sacred ground
on which healing relationships are built."

ᚦᚦᚦ

TEN

HARNESSING THE POWER OF SILENCE: WHEN TO SPEAK AND WHEN TO PAUSE

In the realm of therapy, silence is not merely the absence of speech but a powerful communicative tool that can facilitate deeper introspection, emotional processing, and breakthroughs in understanding. Mastering the use of silence—knowing when to speak and when to pause—requires a nuanced understanding of the therapeutic process and a keen sensitivity to the client's needs and responses. This deliberate use of silence can significantly enhance the efficacy of therapy, providing space for clients to explore their thoughts and feelings in a profound and meaningful way.

Understanding the Functions of Silence in Therapy

Silence in therapy can serve multiple functions, each contributing to the client's journey towards self-awareness and healing. It can be a reflective pause allowing clients to process complex emotions, a respectful space acknowledging the weight of a client's revelations, or a therapeutic tool encouraging clients to articulate their thoughts more deeply.

Reflective Silence: Often, clients need time to think about and absorb the insights that arise during therapy. Silence following a powerful question or statement allows the client to delve deeper into their psyche, exploring feelings and thoughts that surface in the quiet moments. This reflective silence can lead to significant self-discoveries that spoken conversation might not reach.

Supportive Silence: Silence can also be used to communicate support and empathy. After a client shares something particularly emotional or difficult, maintaining silence can be a way to honor their vulnerability and show that the therapist is fully present and engaged, providing space for the emotions to be felt and acknowledged without immediate analysis or response.

Prompting Silence: Used strategically, silence can act as a prompt for the client to continue speaking. In moments where a client may be hesitant to express more complex emotions, a therapist's silence can signal that it is safe to go on and that the therapist is interested in hearing more about the client's experiences and feelings.

Strategies for Effectively Using Silence

Effective use of silence in therapy is as much an art as a science. It requires attunement to the client's verbal and non-verbal cues and a deep understanding of the therapeutic process.

Timing is Key: Knowing when to introduce silence involves reading the emotional and conversational cues during therapy. It is important to gauge whether a client needs time to think or if they are looking for guidance or reassurance. Misjudged silence can feel awkward or unsettling; however, well-timed silence can be immensely powerful.

Creating a Comfortable Space for Silence: For silence to be effective, clients must feel comfortable in it. This comfort can be cultivated over time as the therapeutic relationship strengthens. Therapists can help by normalizing the use of silence, explaining its purpose and value in therapy sessions, and demonstrating comfort with silence themselves.

Observing the Impact: Therapists should closely observe how clients respond to silence. Different clients may react differently; some may find it calming, while others might feel anxious or pressured. These observations can inform how often and how long silence should be used in future sessions.

Using Non-Verbal Communication: During periods of silence, non-verbal cues become even more significant. Maintaining eye contact, adopting an open posture, or nodding slightly can reassure the client that the therapist is engaged and empathetic, providing support without words.

Integrating Silence with Speaking: Balancing silence with verbal communication is crucial. Therapists should be adept at switching smoothly between speaking and pausing, ensuring that both are used effectively to advance the therapeutic goals. Following a period of silence with a summarizing or reflective statement can help validate the client's thoughts and feelings, reinforcing the productive use of silence.

Silence is a powerful tool in the therapeutic toolkit, offering unique ways to deepen the therapy process. When used with intention and sensitivity, it can enhance communication, encourage self-reflection, and facilitate emotional breakthroughs. Mastering the use of silence involves understanding its various functions within therapy, being attuned to the client's needs, and skillfully integrating silent moments with verbal interaction to create a supportive and effective therapeutic environment.

ᐅᐅᐅ

"In the future, therapy will be woven into the fabric of daily life, lessening the stigma and enhancing the access. It will be as much about maintaining mental wellness as it is about treating mental illness."

ᗡᗡᗡ

ELEVEN

REFLECTIVE RESPONSES: MIRRORING FOR UNDERSTANDING

Reflective responses, or mirroring, are a cornerstone technique in therapy that enhances understanding and empathy between the therapist and the client. This approach involves the therapist echoing back to the client what has been said, not merely repeating their words, but reflecting the underlying thoughts, feelings, and meanings.

Through this technique, therapists help clients clarify their thoughts, perceive their feelings more deeply, and feel profoundly understood. This fosters greater self-awareness and can catalyze healing and change.

The Importance of Reflective Responses

Reflective responses serve multiple purposes in therapy. They validate the client's experiences, demonstrate that the therapist is actively listening and engaged, and help to clarify and expand on the client's communication.

By mirroring the client's statements with added insight, therapists can encourage clients to explore their thoughts and emotions further, opening doors to areas that may need attention or that could lead to breakthroughs in therapy.

Validation: When therapists reflect what a client has said, they send a powerful message that the client's feelings and thoughts are important and worthy of attention. This validation is crucial for building self-esteem and can be particularly healing for clients who have felt misunderstood or marginalized in the past.

Clarification: Reflective responses help clients to hear their own thoughts and feelings expressed in another voice, which can help them see things more clearly. This can be particularly useful when clients are confused about their feelings or when they are expressing contradictory emotions.

Deepening Understanding: By adding subtle nuances or emphasizing certain words, therapists can help clients explore deeper layers of their experiences. This technique can guide clients to insights they might not have reached on their own, deepening their understanding of themselves and their relationships.

Techniques in Reflective Responding

Effective reflective responding requires skill and sensitivity. Therapists must tune in to not only the words but also the emotions and body language of the client, and reflect these elements back in a way that adds value to the conversation.

Listening with Empathy: The first step to effective mirroring is empathetic listening. This involves listening with the intent to understand rather than to respond. It requires full attention to the client, not just to their words but also to the nuances of how they speak, their pauses, tone, and body language.

Reflecting Content and Emotion: Good reflective responses rephrase what the client has said and also capture the emotional tone of the message. If a client says, "I just feel so overwhelmed with everything," a reflective response might be, "It sounds like you're carrying a very heavy load right now."

This not only acknowledges the content of what was said but also empathizes with the feeling of being overwhelmed.

Using Summarization: Summarizing is a form of reflective response that involves pulling together several points the client has made, showing how they interconnect, and reflecting them back to provide a broader perspective. This can help clients see patterns in their thoughts or behaviors that they might not have recognized.

Encouraging Elaboration: Sometimes, reflective responses are formulated as questions that encourage further exploration. For instance, if a client expresses difficulty in a relationship, a therapist might reflect, "You seem really hurt by what happened. Can you share more about what that was like for you?"

Adjusting to the Client's Response: Effective use of reflective responses requires observing how the client reacts to them and adjusting accordingly.

If a client responds positively, feeling understood and supported, the therapist might continue in a similar vein. If the client corrects the reflection, this is also valuable as it clarifies their thought process and emotional state.

Reflective responses are a vital therapeutic tool that enhances communication, fosters deeper understanding, and facilitates emotional healing. This technique helps build a supportive therapeutic relationship, where clients feel heard and understood on a deep level, encouraging them to open up and engage more fully in the therapeutic process.

The skillful use of mirroring can significantly impact the effectiveness of therapy, aiding clients in their journey toward self-discovery and personal growth.

❧❧❧

"Self-care for therapists isn't just a practice, it's a necessity. In taking care of ourselves, we ensure we have the capacity to care for others. This balance is the key to sustainable practice."

🖤🖤🖤

TWELVE

COPING WITH TRANSFERENCE: MANAGING EMOTIONAL PROJECTIONS

Transference is a psychological phenomenon that occurs when a client unconsciously redirects or transfers feelings and behaviors they have toward significant people in their past onto the therapist. This can include a range of emotions such as affection, hostility, fear, or dependency. Understanding and managing transference is crucial in therapy because it can provide deep insights into a client's interpersonal relationships and emotional history, but if not handled correctly, it can also hinder the therapeutic process.

Understanding Transference in Therapy

Transference often arises as clients begin to trust and open up in the therapeutic environment, inadvertently placing the therapist into roles that mirror significant relationships from their past. For instance, a client may start to interact with a therapist as they would with a parent, sibling, or former partner, replaying both positive and negative dynamics of these relationships.

Transference is not limited to negative emotions; it can also involve idealization of the therapist, where the client attributes unrealistic abilities or virtues to the therapist, similar to those they might have once ascribed to a caregiver or other influential figure in their life. Both forms of transference can be revealing and serve as a gateway to exploring unresolved issues and patterns in the client's life.

Strategies for Managing Transference

Recognizing Transference: The first step in managing transference is recognizing when it is occurring. This may not always be clear immediately, but certain clues can signal its presence. For instance, if a client's reactions or emotions seem out of proportion to the situation, or if they begin to respond to the therapist based on assumptions that do not align with the therapist's actual behaviors or statements, transference may be at play.

Maintaining Professional Boundaries: Once transference is identified, it is crucial for therapists to maintain clear and consistent professional boundaries. This helps distinguish the therapeutic relationship from other personal relationships in the client's life. Boundaries reinforce the therapist's role as a professional guide rather than a participant in the client's personal life drama.

Addressing Transference Directly: Therapists can address transference directly by gently pointing out to the client when they seem to be reacting to the therapist as if they were someone else from their past. This discussion should be handled with sensitivity and empathy, as it can be unsettling for clients to realize they are transferring feelings onto the therapist.

Exploring the Roots of Transference: Discussing and exploring the origins of transference can be therapeutic in itself. It allows clients to gain insight into their relational patterns and unresolved conflicts. Therapists can guide clients through this exploration, helping them understand how their past relationships are influencing their current emotions and behaviors, including their interactions within the therapeutic setting.

Using Transference as a Therapeutic Tool: When managed effectively, transference can be used as a powerful therapeutic tool. It provides a live context for clients to explore their feelings, expectations, and relational dynamics. Therapists can help clients analyze and process these dynamics as they unfold, which can lead to significant breakthroughs in understanding and resolving past conflicts.

Facilitating Emotional Processing: As clients begin to understand and unravel the emotions involved in transference, therapists can facilitate emotional processing. This involves helping clients express and work through the complex feelings that have surfaced, providing them with strategies to manage these emotions both within and outside of therapy sessions.

Encouraging Self-reflection: Encouraging clients to reflect on their experiences of transference can enhance their self-awareness and contribute to personal growth. This reflection can be facilitated through therapeutic techniques such as journaling, mindfulness, and discussion of therapy sessions.

Transference is a common, yet complex, phenomenon in therapy that requires careful navigation. Recognizing, addressing, and utilizing transference effectively are key components of therapeutic work. When managed well, transference not only enriches the therapeutic process by providing valuable insights into a client's inner world and past relationships but also fosters deeper healing and a more profound understanding of oneself.

ᔕᔕᔕ

"Every therapy session is a chance for renewal and discovery. Each conversation is a step towards understanding, and every insight a light in the darkness."

ʕʕʕ

THIRTEEN

Ethical Considerations: Integrity in Every Interaction

Ethics in therapy encompass a broad spectrum of considerations that ensure the integrity and effectiveness of the therapeutic process. These ethical considerations are crucial for maintaining professional boundaries, ensuring client welfare, and providing high-quality mental health services. Integrity in every interaction is not just an ideal to strive for but a fundamental requirement that underpins the entire therapeutic relationship and process.

Core Ethical Principles in Therapy

Confidentiality: Confidentiality is paramount in therapy, as it protects client privacy and fosters a safe space for open communication. Therapists must safeguard information shared by clients during sessions, only breaking confidentiality in situations where there is a risk of harm to the client or others, as mandated by law. This ethical principle reassures clients that their disclosures are protected, encouraging honesty and vulnerability in the therapeutic setting.

Informed Consent: Clients have the right to be fully informed about their treatment, including the methods used, the duration expected, and the costs involved. Informed consent also includes informing clients about the limits of confidentiality and how their information will be handled. This transparency is essential for building trust and ensuring that clients feel respected and in control of their treatment process.

Non-maleficence and Beneficence: These twin principles involve, respectively, doing no harm and working actively to do good for the client. Therapists must be diligent in ensuring that their interventions do not harm clients and that their actions are aimed at promoting client welfare. This involves staying well-informed about the best practices in therapy and constantly evaluating the effectiveness and appropriateness of treatments.

Competence: Therapists are ethically obliged to provide services for which they are qualified through education, training, and experience. Maintaining competence includes ongoing professional development and self-awareness to prevent conditions such as burnout, which could impair their performance. Therapists must also recognize the limits of their expertise and refer clients to other professionals when appropriate.

Autonomy: Respecting client autonomy involves acknowledging their right to make decisions about their therapeutic journey. This means supporting clients in making informed decisions about their treatment options and respecting their choices, even when these differ from the therapist's views. It also involves empowering clients by fostering their independence and self-determination.

Navigating Ethical Challenges in Therapy

Dealing with ethical challenges in therapy requires a careful and thoughtful approach. Therapists must be adept at identifying potential ethical dilemmas and employing strategies to resolve them responsibly.

Dual Relationships: Managing dual relationships — where the therapist and the client have another form of relationship outside of therapy — can be particularly challenging. Therapists must strive to avoid such relationships as they can create conflicts of interest and blur the boundaries of the professional relationship. If a dual relationship is unavoidable, it should be navigated with clear boundaries and transparency, always prioritizing the client's best interests.

Cultural Sensitivity: Ethical practice also involves being culturally sensitive and aware of diversity in all its forms. Therapists should strive to understand the cultural background of their clients and consider how cultural factors influence the therapeutic process. This includes being aware of and challenging one's own biases and ensuring that therapy is culturally appropriate and respectful.

Handling Confidentiality Breaches: In cases where confidentiality must be breached — for instance, if there is a threat to the client or others — therapists must handle the situation with care. This involves informing the client about the breach, if possible, and taking steps to ensure that the information is disclosed only to the necessary extent.

Dealing with Unethical Behavior: If therapists encounter unethical behavior within their profession, whether in colleagues or within the institutions they work with, they are ethically obligated to address it. This might involve reporting the behavior to the appropriate authorities or professional bodies, always with the aim of protecting clients and maintaining the integrity of the profession.

Ethics are foundational to the practice of therapy, guiding therapists in conducting their professional duties with integrity, respect, and compassion. Adhering to ethical principles not only protects clients but also enhances the therapeutic relationship and the effectiveness of therapy. Through diligent ethical practice, therapists contribute to the overall credibility and trustworthiness of the mental health profession.

ϷϷϷ

"In therapy, sometimes silence speaks louder than
words. It's in these moments of quiet that the
deepest reflections and realizations can occur.
Silence is not empty; it's full of answers."

ppp

FOURTEEN

BUILDING RESILIENCE: ENCOURAGING STRENGTH AND ADAPTABILITY

Resilience in the context of psychology is the ability to bounce back from setbacks, adapt well to change, and keep going in the face of adversity. Building resilience is a fundamental aspect of therapy, as it empowers clients not only to cope with current difficulties but also to handle future challenges more effectively. Encouraging strength and adaptability in clients involves a combination of strategies aimed at enhancing their coping mechanisms, fostering a positive outlook, and strengthening their emotional and psychological fortitude.

Understanding Resilience

Resilience is not a trait that people either have or do not have.

It involves behaviors, thoughts, and actions that can be learned and developed by anyone. A resilient individual is able to approach problems flexibly, maintain emotional balance in stressful situations, and recover from or adjust easily to misfortune or change. For therapists, building resilience in clients is about nurturing these capacities through therapeutic interventions.

Components of Resilience

Emotional Awareness: Understanding and managing one's emotions are crucial for resilience. Therapy can help clients identify and articulate their emotions, which is a key step in learning to handle them effectively. Emotional awareness also includes recognizing how emotions affect behavior and decision-making.

Perseverance: Often, resilience involves an element of perseverance through difficult or complex situations. Therapy can support clients in developing a mindset that focuses on persistence, helping them understand that setbacks are temporary and surmountable.

Optimism: Maintaining a hopeful outlook is a powerful part of resilience. Optimism doesn't mean ignoring the reality of a situation but rather maintaining a mindset that, despite current difficulties, the future can be better. Therapists can encourage clients to cultivate an optimistic outlook by focusing on solutions and possibilities rather than dwelling excessively on problems.

Flexibility: Resilient individuals can adapt to changing circumstances and stressors effectively. In therapy, clients can learn to develop flexibility not only by adjusting their behaviors in response to external situations but also by modifying their internal expectations and attitudes.

Support Networks: Building and relying on a healthy support network is essential for resilience. Therapy can help clients recognize the value of seeking help and strengthen their relationships with friends, family, and community resources.

Strategies for Building Resilience

Building resilience is an ongoing process that can be integrated into various aspects of therapeutic practice. Here are some strategies that therapists can use to help clients develop resilience:

Cognitive Behavioral Techniques: These techniques are effective in changing pessimistic or negative thought patterns that can impede resilience. By challenging and reframing irrational or maladaptive thoughts, clients can develop more realistic and positive thinking patterns.

Stress Reduction Techniques: Teaching clients how to manage stress effectively is crucial for building resilience. Techniques such as mindfulness, meditation, deep breathing exercises, and physical relaxation can help reduce the impact of stress on emotional and physical health.

Problem-Solving Skills: Resilient people are often effective problem solvers. By teaching clients how to assess problems, generate options, and take decisive actions, therapists can enhance their clients' ability to deal with challenges constructively.

Goal Setting: Helping clients set and achieve goals can foster a sense of accomplishment and purpose, which are important for resilience. Goals should be specific, measurable, attainable, relevant, and time-bound (SMART), and strategies should be put in place to deal with potential obstacles.

Narrative Therapy: This therapeutic approach involves helping clients reframe and reinterpret their life stories from a resilience perspective. By focusing on their strengths and successes, clients can see themselves as resilient individuals, which can be empowering and transformative.

Encouragement of Self-Care: Promoting healthy practices such as good nutrition, regular exercise, and adequate sleep is essential in building resilience. These practices enhance physical well-being, which supports mental health.

Building resilience is a key objective of therapeutic intervention. It involves a multifaceted approach that enhances the client's capacity to cope with adversity, adapt to change, and emerge stronger from challenges. By focusing on developing emotional awareness, perseverance, optimism, flexibility, and strong social supports, therapy can play a crucial role in fostering resilience, ultimately enabling clients to lead healthier, more fulfilling lives.

❤❤❤

"Building resilience in clients is like planting seeds in a garden. It requires patience, care, and the right conditions to grow. Over time, these seeds become strong enough to weather any storm."

❦❦❦

FIFTEEN

Crisis Intervention: Immediate Actions and Lasting Solutions

Crisis intervention in therapy is a vital component of mental health care, focusing on immediate assistance and stabilization for individuals who are experiencing acute psychological distress. A crisis can arise from a variety of situations, including traumatic events, sudden losses, severe health diagnoses, or significant life changes. Effective crisis intervention not only addresses the immediate problem but also lays the groundwork for sustainable coping strategies and long-term recovery.

Understanding the Nature of a Crisis

A crisis is characterized by an individual's inability to cope effectively with a particular stressor, leading to a state of emotional turmoil. This turmoil can disrupt their ability to function normally in daily life, presenting a risk to their well-being and requiring immediate and skilled intervention. The primary goals of crisis intervention are to mitigate the impact of the event, restore safety, and assist the individual in returning to their baseline functioning, or better.

Principles of Effective Crisis Intervention

Effective crisis intervention is guided by several core principles that prioritize safety, rapid response, and individual needs:

Safety First: The initial step in any crisis intervention is to ensure the physical and psychological safety of the individual. This may involve addressing any immediate risks to safety, including harm to oneself or others. Establishing a safe environment is crucial for reducing stress and enabling the individual to engage in further therapeutic interventions.

Validation of Experience: It is essential to acknowledge and validate the individual's feelings and experiences without judgment. This validation provides emotional relief and reassures the individual that their responses are understood and taken seriously, fostering a trusting therapeutic relationship.

Stabilization: Stabilization involves calming the individual and providing support to reduce symptoms of distress. Techniques might include breathing exercises, grounding techniques, or other immediate coping strategies that can help lower anxiety and distress levels.

Assessment: Conducting a thorough assessment is critical to understanding the specific needs and risks associated with the crisis. This includes exploring the nature of the crisis, the individual's mental health history, current coping mechanisms, and available support systems. An accurate assessment will guide the subsequent steps in the intervention and treatment planning.

Crisis Planning: Developing a crisis response plan that includes practical steps the individual can take if symptoms escalate is crucial. This plan should be clearly outlined and accessible, providing concrete strategies and contacts in case of emergency.

Referral and Support: Often, additional resources such as community services, support groups, or ongoing therapy may be necessary. Referring individuals to these resources ensures they receive comprehensive care and supports the transition from immediate crisis intervention to long-term recovery.

Strategies for Immediate Actions

When addressing a crisis, specific immediate actions are tailored to the individual's emotional and physical state and the nature of the crisis:

Active Listening: Listening attentively to the individual's concerns without interruption is vital in crisis situations. It helps the therapist to gather important information and demonstrates empathy and respect for the individual's experience.

Direct Communication: Clear, direct communication is essential during a crisis. Information should be straightforward to reduce misunderstandings and help clarify the situation for the individual, who may be confused or overwhelmed.

Psychological First Aid: This involves providing emotional comfort and practical assistance. Techniques might include helping the individual to name their emotions, offering reassurance, or facilitating access to immediate physical needs like shelter or medical care.

Building Towards Lasting Solutions

Transitioning from immediate crisis intervention to longer-term solutions involves:

Therapeutic Intervention: Once stabilization is achieved, more in-depth therapeutic techniques can be employed to address underlying issues and reinforce coping strategies. These may include cognitive-behavioral therapy, trauma-focused interventions, or other modalities suited to the individual's needs.

Building Resilience: Enhancing resilience through therapy can help individuals better manage future stresses. This might involve developing problem-solving skills, strengthening social supports, and fostering adaptive coping mechanisms.

Monitoring and Follow-Up: Regular follow-ups are important to assess recovery progress, make adjustments to the treatment plan, and provide ongoing support. Monitoring helps ensure that the individual remains on track and continues to find effective strategies for managing stress and avoiding future crises.

Crisis intervention requires immediate and skillful responses that prioritize safety, rapid stabilization, and empathetic care. By effectively addressing both the immediate distress and the underlying issues, therapists can help individuals recover from crises and build stronger, more resilient futures.

ᐅᐅᐅ

"The therapist's journey is one of constant learning and loving empathy. With every client's story, we weave another thread into the broader human tapestry. This work is not just a profession; it's a privilege."

ᐁᐁᐁ

SIXTEEN

THE HEALING POTENTIAL OF HUMOR: LIGHTENING THE LOAD

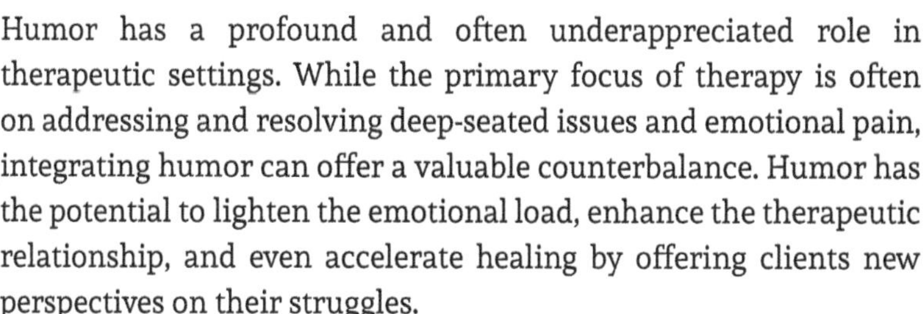

Humor has a profound and often underappreciated role in therapeutic settings. While the primary focus of therapy is often on addressing and resolving deep-seated issues and emotional pain, integrating humor can offer a valuable counterbalance. Humor has the potential to lighten the emotional load, enhance the therapeutic relationship, and even accelerate healing by offering clients new perspectives on their struggles.

Understanding the Role of Humor in Therapy

Humor in therapy does not mean making light of serious issues or using laughter to deflect from important emotional work. Rather, it is about using humor as a strategic tool to help clients confront difficult realities in ways that are less threatening and more accessible. When used appropriately, humor can be a powerful adjunct to traditional therapeutic techniques, providing relief and a sense of normalcy in the often intense environment of therapy.

Benefits of Humor in Therapy

Reduces Stress and Anxiety: Humor is a well-known stress reliever. Laughter triggers the release of endorphins, the body's natural feel-good chemicals. It promotes an overall sense of well-being and can temporarily relieve pain. By reducing stress and anxiety, humor can make clients more receptive to therapy and open to discussing their issues.

Strengthens the Therapeutic Alliance: Sharing a laugh can create a stronger bond between therapist and client. This bonding can enhance trust and make clients feel more comfortable sharing sensitive information. Humor can humanize the therapist, breaking down barriers of formality and creating a more egalitarian therapeutic relationship.

Encourages a Shift in Perspective: Humor can help clients see their situations in new ways. A humorous remark might reframe a problem or highlight the absurdity of a situation, which can be enlightening and freeing. This shift can empower clients to approach their issues from a different angle or with a new mindset that is less burdened by emotional weight.

Facilitates Resilience: By fostering a lighter, more optimistic atmosphere, humor can help clients build resilience. Laughing in the face of challenges can be an act of defiance against the hardships of life, promoting a sense of strength and control. This resilience is crucial for clients as they work through their issues and beyond, helping them manage future stresses with a healthier outlook.

Integrating Humor into Therapeutic Practice

Incorporating humor into therapy must be done thoughtfully and sensitively, with a clear understanding of the client's preferences, cultural background, and emotional state. Here are some strategies for therapists looking to integrate humor into their sessions:

Assess Suitability: Not every client or situation is appropriate for the use of humor. Therapists must assess whether humor will be beneficial or could potentially harm the therapeutic process. This assessment should be ongoing, as the appropriateness of humor may change over the course of therapy.

Follow the Client's Lead: The safest way to introduce humor is to follow the client's lead. If a client makes a humorous comment, echoing their humor can reinforce the behavior and signal that levity is acceptable in the therapeutic space.

Use Self-deprecating Humor: Therapists using self-deprecating humor can model for clients how to take themselves less seriously. This type of humor must be used carefully to avoid undermining the therapist's credibility but can effectively lighten the mood and make the therapist more relatable.

Highlight the Absurdities: Pointing out the absurdities in situations or in the client's thinking can be a gentle way to introduce humor. This must be done delicately to ensure that the client feels understood and not mocked.

Incorporate Playful Techniques: Techniques such as playful role-play or humor-filled metaphors can introduce lightness and fun into the session, helping clients tackle serious issues in a less daunting way.

Educate About the Benefits of Laughter: Sometimes, simply educating clients about the physiological and psychological benefits of laughter can encourage them to embrace humor outside of therapy, enhancing their overall quality of life.

When used appropriately, humor can be a valuable tool in therapy, providing a myriad of benefits including stress reduction, enhanced therapeutic alliances, new perspectives, and increased resilience. By carefully integrating humor into their practice, therapists can help clients navigate their therapeutic journeys with a bit more ease and optimism, making the path toward healing a little lighter.

ᐅᐅᐅ

"Teletherapy has bridged the gap between need and
access, bringing the therapeutic conversation into
homes and hearts. It proves that healing doesn't
have a set stage—it follows wherever it is needed."

❥❥❥

SEVENTEEN

CULTURAL SENSITIVITY: HONORING DIVERSE BACKGROUNDS

Cultural sensitivity in therapy is essential for providing effective and respectful treatment that honors the diverse backgrounds of clients. It involves understanding, appreciating, and integrating clients' cultural values, beliefs, and behaviors into the therapeutic process. This approach not only enhances the therapeutic relationship but also promotes better outcomes by aligning treatment with the client's own cultural context and identity.

Importance of Cultural Sensitivity in Therapy

Cultural sensitivity is crucial because it affects how clients perceive and interact with the therapeutic process. A lack of cultural awareness can lead to misunderstandings, decreased effectiveness of treatment, and even harm. By being culturally sensitive, therapists demonstrate respect for the client's background, which helps build trust and openness in the therapeutic relationship.

Challenges of Cultural Sensitivity

Diverse Client Backgrounds: Therapists encounter clients from a wide range of cultural backgrounds, including differences in ethnicity, nationality, religion, sexual orientation, and socioeconomic status, among others. Each of these factors can influence how clients understand and cope with mental health issues.

Avoiding Cultural Assumptions: It is important for therapists to avoid assumptions based on a client's cultural background. Stereotyping can lead to misinterpretations and oversimplifications of the client's experiences and needs.

Cultural Taboos and Stigma: Mental health stigma varies significantly across cultures, and what is considered a normal emotional expression in one culture may be taboo in another. Therapists must navigate these differences to effectively engage clients and encourage them to open up about their feelings and experiences.

Strategies for Cultivating Cultural Sensitivity

Cultural Competence Training: Ongoing education and training in cultural competence can equip therapists with the knowledge and skills needed to understand and appropriately respond to the cultural contexts of their clients. This training often includes learning about different cultural practices, communication styles, and health beliefs that affect therapy.

Self-Awareness: Therapists must be aware of their own cultural backgrounds and biases, understanding how these influence their perceptions and interactions with clients. Reflecting on one's own cultural identity and biases can help therapists avoid imposing their values on clients.

Client-Centered Approach: Placing the client at the center of therapy means actively listening to their experiences and allowing their cultural identity to inform the therapeutic process. This approach respects the client's perspective and integrates their cultural values and practices into treatment planning.

Use of Culturally Adapted Treatment Models: Therapists should consider adapting treatment models to better fit the cultural context of the client. This might involve modifying therapeutic techniques to align with cultural norms and values or incorporating culturally significant symbols and practices into therapy.

Language and Communication Style: Being sensitive to language and communication styles is crucial. This may involve using a client's first language if possible or being mindful of non-verbal communication cues that vary by culture. Therapists might also need to adjust their delivery of therapy to match the client's communication preferences, such as storytelling or a more formal dialogue style.

Collaboration with Community Resources: Engaging with community leaders and resources can enhance cultural sensitivity. This might involve consulting with cultural experts or community organizations that can provide insight into the client's cultural background and current community dynamics.

Feedback and Adaptation: Encouraging feedback from clients about the cultural relevance and sensitivity of the therapy they receive is vital. This feedback can guide therapists in making necessary adjustments to better meet the cultural and individual needs of their clients.

Cultural sensitivity is a fundamental aspect of effective therapy. It requires a commitment to ongoing education, self-reflection, and adaptability on the part of the therapist. By honoring and integrating the diverse cultural backgrounds of their clients, therapists can build stronger therapeutic relationships and provide more effective, respectful, and personalized care. This approach not only enhances individual therapy outcomes but also contributes to the broader goal of making mental health services accessible and relevant to all segments of society.

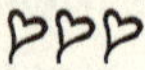

"Reviewing progress in therapy is like mapping the journey of a thousand miles. It shows us how far we've come, not just in distance, but in growth. This reflection is both a celebration and a guide for the road ahead."

❦❦❦

EIGHTEEN

Ending Therapy: Timelines and Techniques for Closure

Ending therapy is a critical phase of the therapeutic process, marking a period of reflection, integration, and planning for the future. Whether a client's therapy concludes due to planned termination or other circumstances, it is vital to approach this phase with care. Effective closure helps ensure that the client feels a sense of accomplishment and is equipped to manage independently, sustaining the progress made during therapy.

Understanding the Importance of Closure in Therapy

Proper closure in therapy is as crucial as any other stage of the therapeutic process. It allows both the client and therapist to reflect on the journey, acknowledge growth, and address any remaining concerns. It also prepares the client for the end of the therapy relationship, which can be a significant transition, especially if therapy has been long-term.

Determining When to End Therapy

The decision to end therapy can be driven by various factors including the achievement of therapeutic goals, changes in the client's life, financial factors, or feeling that the client is ready to continue their growth independently. It is important for this decision to be made collaboratively, involving open discussion between therapist and client about readiness and feelings regarding termination.

Techniques for Effective Closure

Reviewing Progress: One of the first steps in effective closure is reviewing the client's progress. This review can involve discussing the goals set at the beginning of therapy, achievements made, and obstacles overcome. This reflection not only reinforces the client's growth but also helps consolidate the skills and strategies learned during therapy.

Addressing Unfinished Business: It is important to identify any unresolved issues and decide how to handle them. If there are outstanding topics that need more attention, the therapist and client may agree on strategies for addressing these post-therapy or consider extending the sessions to cover these areas more fully.

Planning for the Future: Discussing strategies for maintaining and continuing progress post-therapy is crucial. This might involve creating a relapse prevention plan, identifying signs of backsliding, and deciding what steps to take if challenges re-emerge. Clients should feel equipped with the tools and strategies needed to handle potential stressors independently.

Celebrating Achievements: Recognizing and celebrating the changes and improvements made during therapy can be very empowering for clients. This celebration helps to solidify the client's sense of self-efficacy and accomplishment.

Processing Feelings About Ending Therapy: It is natural for clients to have mixed emotions about ending therapy. They may feel proud of their progress yet anxious about losing the support of their therapist. Therapists can facilitate discussions that help clients process these feelings, validating their experiences and encouraging them to express any concerns or fears.

Ensuring Continuity of Care: If necessary, therapists should provide referrals to other professionals or resources to ensure that clients continue to receive support, especially if they are still dealing with significant issues or challenges. Ensuring continuity of care is particularly important in cases where clients require ongoing support for mental health issues.

Final Session Rituals: Many therapists use rituals or symbolic activities in the final session to signify the end of the therapy journey. This could be a special closing activity, such as writing a goodbye letter, creating a list of key insights learned, or setting future goals.

Follow-Up Sessions: Some therapists offer follow-up sessions after the official termination of regular sessions. These sessions can provide additional support as clients adjust to managing independently and can serve as a safety net to catch any potential problems early.

The Role of the Therapist in Facilitating Closure

The therapist plays a crucial role in facilitating a smooth and therapeutic ending to the therapy relationship. This involves being proactive in planning for the end of therapy, transparent in discussions about termination, and sensitive to the emotional impact of ending the therapeutic relationship. Therapists should strive to make the process as positive and empowering as possible, reinforcing the client's ability to succeed beyond the therapy setting.

The end of therapy is a significant phase that requires careful handling to ensure it is a positive, affirming experience. By effectively reviewing progress, addressing any remaining issues, celebrating achievements, and planning for future challenges, therapists can help clients feel prepared and confident as they transition out of regular therapy sessions. This approach not only honors the work done during the therapeutic process but also supports clients in maintaining and building on their gains independently.

ᎭᎭᎭ

"The end of therapy is not the end of growth. It's a
new beginning, a testament to the client's readiness
to apply their newfound strengths. As therapists,
our goal is to make ourselves obsolete, empowering
clients to stand on their own."

ppp

NINETEEN

SUPERVISION AND SELF-CARE: SUSTAINING THE CAREGIVER

For therapists and caregivers, the dual practices of supervision and self-care are essential to sustain their ability to provide effective, empathetic care while maintaining their own well-being. These practices are not just beneficial but necessary, as the demands of caregiving and therapy can lead to burnout, compassion fatigue, and secondary traumatic stress if not managed properly. Understanding and implementing effective strategies for supervision and self-care can help sustain caregivers throughout their careers.

The Importance of Supervision

Supervision in therapy refers to a structured process wherein less experienced therapists or caregivers receive guidance, support, and education from more experienced colleagues. This process is crucial for several reasons:

Enhancing Clinical Skills: Supervision provides an opportunity for caregivers to refine their therapeutic techniques, expand their knowledge base, and improve their ability to diagnose and treat clients. It allows for the review of case studies, discussion of therapeutic strategies, and feedback on handling difficult situations.

Ethical Guidance: Supervisors play a key role in helping therapists navigate complex ethical dilemmas that may arise during therapy. This guidance ensures that caregivers maintain professional boundaries and adhere to ethical standards, safeguarding the welfare of both the client and the therapist.

Emotional Support and Processing: Therapy can be emotionally taxing. Supervisors offer a space for therapists to process their feelings about their work, discuss personal reactions to clients, and explore any countertransference issues. This emotional support is vital to prevent emotional overload and burnout.

Professional Development: Regular supervision aids in continual professional growth and learning, keeping therapists updated on new research and developments in the field. It also helps therapists set and achieve career goals, enhancing job satisfaction and effectiveness.

Self-Care Strategies for Caregivers

Self-care involves activities and practices that therapists undertake to maintain their health, well-being, and effectiveness as clinicians. Effective self-care strategies are personalized and require regular practice. Key aspects include:

Physical Health: Caregivers should prioritize their physical health by maintaining a balanced diet, getting regular exercise, and ensuring adequate sleep. Physical well-being significantly impacts mental health and the ability to cope with stress.

Emotional Well-being: Engaging in hobbies and activities outside of work helps maintain emotional balance. Therapists often benefit from their own therapy or counseling to manage the emotional demands of their work.

Social Support: Maintaining strong personal relationships and a supportive social network can provide emotional sustenance and a sense of belonging. Social activities can offer a necessary break and a fun outlet from the pressures of work.

Professional Boundaries: Setting and adhering to clear professional boundaries helps prevent burnout. This includes managing work hours, taking regular breaks, and ensuring there is a separation between personal and professional life.

Mindfulness and Relaxation Techniques: Practices such as meditation, yoga, and mindfulness can reduce stress and enhance overall well-being. Regular practice helps maintain a calm, centered approach to both personal challenges and professional responsibilities.

Continual Learning and Growth: Engaging in continuous education and personal development can keep the work interesting and intellectually stimulating. This might include attending workshops, conferences, and pursuing further education.

Scheduled Downtime: It's important for therapists to schedule downtime explicitly. This includes vacations as well as regular, shorter periods of time away from work to relax and rejuvenate.

Reflection and Journaling: Regular reflection on one's work through journaling or other forms of self-exploration can provide insights into personal growth and effectiveness as a therapist.

Integrating Supervision and Self-Care

Integrating both supervision and self-care into the routine of a caregiver creates a robust framework for sustaining long-term effectiveness and personal well-being. Supervision provides external support and insight, while self-care allows for internal consolidation and recovery. Together, these practices ensure that caregivers can continue to provide compassionate and effective care without sacrificing their own health and happiness.

The integration of supervision and self-care into the life of a caregiver is not merely an optional addition but a crucial element of a sustainable career in therapy. These practices are interdependent, each reinforcing the other to create a more resilient, effective, and fulfilled caregiver. By prioritizing both, therapists can protect themselves from the hazards of their profession and enhance their capacity to help others.

ᐯᐯᐯ

"*The future of therapy lies in its ability to adapt—to technologies, to evolving societal norms, and to the ever-changing landscapes of mental health. The core, however, remains unchanged: the profound, healing connection between therapist and client.*"

❦❦❦

TWENTY

FUTURE DIRECTIONS: EVOLVING PRACTICES IN THERAPY

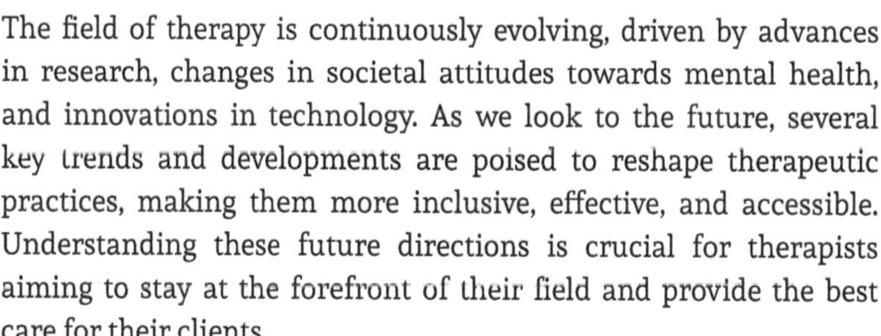

The field of therapy is continuously evolving, driven by advances in research, changes in societal attitudes towards mental health, and innovations in technology. As we look to the future, several key trends and developments are poised to reshape therapeutic practices, making them more inclusive, effective, and accessible. Understanding these future directions is crucial for therapists aiming to stay at the forefront of their field and provide the best care for their clients.

Integration of Technology

One of the most significant changes in therapy has been the integration of technology. Teletherapy, the practice of conducting therapy sessions through digital platforms, has become increasingly popular, particularly highlighted by its essential role during the COVID-19 pandemic. This mode of delivery is not only convenient but also expands access to therapy for those in remote areas or with mobility issues. Looking ahead, we can expect further advancements in this area, such as the use of artificial intelligence (AI) to tailor therapeutic interventions to individual clients or to provide supplemental support between sessions.

Enhanced Focus on Multicultural Competence

As societies become more diverse, the need for culturally competent therapy has never been more critical. Future trends in therapy emphasize understanding and integrating multiple cultural perspectives into practice. This includes not only broadening the cultural knowledge base of therapists but also adopting a more nuanced approach to how cultural, societal, and personal identities interact and affect mental health. Training programs and continuing education courses are increasingly focusing on multicultural competence, preparing therapists to work effectively in a globalized world.

Expansion of Evidence-Based Practices

The future of therapy is also marked by an increased reliance on evidence-based practices (EBPs). These practices, grounded in rigorous research and clinical trials, ensure that the therapeutic interventions provided have been proven effective. As research continues to evolve, therapists must stay informed about the latest developments and integrate new and effective strategies into their practice. Additionally, there is a growing trend towards personalizing these practices to fit individual client needs, moving away from a one-size-fits-all approach.

Preventative Mental Health Care

There is a growing recognition of the importance of preventative mental health care. Future therapeutic practices are likely to focus more on early intervention, aiming to address mental health issues before they develop into more severe disorders. This approach not only helps reduce the prevalence of mental health conditions but also lessens the overall burden on healthcare systems. Schools, workplaces, and community centers are increasingly seen as important venues for delivering preventive mental health strategies.

Interdisciplinary Approaches

The intersection of psychology with other fields such as neuroscience, endocrinology, and immunology is enriching our understanding of the biopsychosocial model of health. Future directions in therapy involve more interdisciplinary approaches that consider a person's mental health within the larger context of their physical health and overall lifestyle. This holistic approach can lead to more comprehensive care and better outcomes for clients.

Increased Client Empowerment

Future trends also emphasize greater client empowerment, involving clients more actively in their treatment planning and decision-making processes. This shift recognizes clients as partners in therapy rather than passive recipients of care. Tools such as mobile health apps, wearable technology, and online resources can support clients in managing their mental health more autonomously, providing them with real-time data and feedback about their psychological state.

Ethical Considerations in Evolving Practices

With these advances, there are also new ethical considerations to address. The use of digital tools raises questions about privacy and data security, while AI in therapy prompts debates about the limits of technology in human-centered professions. Therapists must navigate these challenges carefully, ensuring they adhere to ethical standards and protect their clients' welfare.

The future of therapy holds promising developments that are likely to enhance therapeutic effectiveness and accessibility. By embracing technological advancements, integrating evidence-based practices, focusing on preventative care, and fostering client empowerment, therapists can significantly impact the well-being of their clients. Staying informed and adaptable will be key for therapists aiming to utilize these evolving practices effectively and ethically.

ᗡᗡᗡ

"Crisis intervention is the art of turning chaos into order, despair into hope. It requires swift action but also deep compassion, as the wounds most hidden are often the ones most profound. In these critical moments, we are not just therapists; we are lifelines."

ppp

TWENTY-ONE
SUMMARY

In the ever-evolving field of therapy, the essence of meaningful therapeutic interaction lies at the heart of effective practice. This book, "Secret of Healing Conversations: Nurturing Principles in Counseling and Therapy," serves as an exhaustive guide to mastering the art of therapeutic communication, emphasizing the significance of nurturing principles that foster deep healing and growth. Each chapter delves into a different aspect of therapeutic interaction, building a comprehensive framework that therapists can use to enhance their practice and the lives of their clients.

Active Listening and Empathy

The foundational skills of active listening and empathy are extensively discussed as the bedrock of therapeutic communication. Active listening involves more than just hearing words; it is about engaging with and understanding the client's underlying emotions and thoughts. Empathy goes a step further to connect emotionally with clients, making them feel seen and valued. These skills are crucial for creating a safe and trusting environment where clients can open up and explore their vulnerabilities.

Creating Safe Spaces and Building Trust

Creating a safe, non-judgmental space is essential for effective therapy. This includes not only the physical environment but also the emotional and psychological atmosphere. Establishing trust with clients involves consistent and respectful practices that reassure clients about their privacy and the confidentiality of their disclosures. Trust is a critical component that encourages openness and honesty in therapeutic sessions.

The Power of Validation and Questioning Techniques

Validation affirms the client's feelings and experiences, fostering a sense of acceptance and understanding. This is vital for clients who may have felt misunderstood or marginalized in other areas of their lives. Alongside validation, skillful questioning helps unearth deeper insights into the client's thoughts and behaviors, promoting critical reflection and self-awareness. Questions must be thoughtfully crafted to encourage exploration without leading the client to predetermined conclusions.

Handling Transference and Countertransference

The complexities of transference and countertransference are explored with an emphasis on how therapists can effectively manage these dynamics. Understanding these phenomena is key to decoding the deeper emotional currents of the therapeutic relationship. Properly addressing transference enhances therapeutic work, using it as a tool to gain insight into the client's past relationships and unresolved conflicts.

The Role of Humor and Cultural Sensitivity

Humor, when used judiciously, can lighten the emotional load, making therapy a less daunting experience for clients. It can foster resilience and provide a fresh perspective on difficult issues. Equally important is cultural sensitivity, which involves acknowledging and respecting the client's cultural background. This sensitivity enriches the therapeutic process, making interventions more relevant and effective.

Ethical Considerations

Ethical practice is a thread that runs through all aspects of therapy, from maintaining confidentiality to handling ethical dilemmas that arise during therapy. Ethical considerations are crucial for professional conduct and maintaining the integrity of therapeutic practice. Therapists are urged to stay informed about ethical guidelines and continuously reflect on their practice to ensure they are acting in the best interest of their clients.

Future Directions in Therapy

Looking ahead, the book discusses the future directions of therapeutic practice, including the integration of technology in therapy, the importance of evidence-based practices, and the ongoing need for cultural competence. Advances in technology such as teletherapy and artificial intelligence are making therapy more accessible and potentially more tailored to individual needs.

The guidance in this book encapsulates a holistic approach to the art of therapy. It stresses the importance of each interaction in the therapeutic journey, offering detailed insights and practical strategies to enhance the efficacy of therapy. The book is designed not only to educate new and aspiring therapists but also to serve as a resource for seasoned practitioners looking to deepen their understanding of therapeutic communication. It advocates for a compassionate, empathetic, and scientifically informed approach to therapy, emphasizing that the true power of therapy lies in the quality of connections formed between therapist and client. Through these nurturing principles, therapists are equipped to facilitate real and lasting change, helping clients navigate their pathways to healing and growth.

ﬞﬞﬞ

Citation And References

This book represents the culmination of extensive research and meticulous analysis, incorporating a diverse range of sources, including numerous books, scholarly studies, and personal experiences. Additionally, I have scoured various websites to gather relevant information and data essential for the compilation of this work. I have taken every precaution to ensure the accuracy of the information presented and have diligently cited all sources to acknowledge their contributions.

Despite these efforts, the possibility of inadvertent errors remains. I deeply value the insights of my readers and appreciate any feedback that can help identify and rectify such inaccuracies. I encourage you to bring any discrepancies to my attention.

Your feedback is not only welcome but crucial, as it will aid in correcting current editions and enhancing the content of future ones. I am committed to maintaining the highest standards of accuracy and reliability in my work and thank you for your support and understanding.

Additionally, I firmly uphold the principle of freedom of speech and expression as guaranteed under Article 19(1)(a) of the Constitution of India, and I respect the diverse viewpoints and expressions of all readers.

ppp

Other Books Of The Author

1. Empowering Minds: A Journey into Women's Self-Discovery and Power
2. The Dynamics of Motivation: Catalyzing Thought into Action
3. Meditation and Mental Well Being: The Path to Inner Peace and Clarity
4. The Psychology of Child Education: Nurturing Future Generations
5. Ethical Enlightenment: A Modern Guide to Living with Integrity
6. Voices of Empowerment: Stories of Women Rising Against Odds
7. Social Psychology in Everyday Life: Understanding Human Connections
8. The Essence of Motivational Speaking: Inspiring Change in Others
9. Balancing Acts: Women, Work, and the Will to Lead
10. Guiding with Grace: Raising Children with Compassion and Awareness
11. The Power of Positive Aging: Embracing Life After Fifty
12. Building Resilient Communities: Social Work in Action
13. The Ethical Educator: Principles for Teaching and Learning
14. From Insight to Impact: Social Psychology for a Better World
15. The Ethics of Empathy: A Guide to Ethical Living
16. The Science of Empowering the Self: Navigating Life's Challenges with Psychological Wisdom
17. The Mindful Conscious Leader: Meditation Techniques for Modern Management
18. Pioneering Spirit: Women's Pathways to Leadership and Empowerment
19. Feeling to Healing: The Role of Emotional Intelligence in Child Development
20. Transformative Talks and Words of Inspiration: Insights into Motivational Oratory

21. The Hidden Path to Ethical Sustainability: Crafting a Greener Tomorrow
22. Spiritual Integrity: Navigating Life with Moral Compassion
23. Clean Living, Clean Society: The Ethics of Cleanliness
24. Patriotic Spirits: Building a Nation on Positive Attitudes
25. Innovative Integrity & Vibrant Visions: The Ethical and Entrepreneurial Spirit of Gujarat
26. Youthful Visions, Endless Possibilities: Inspiring Ethics and Motivation in Children
27. Living Your Legacy: How to Motivate Others by Living Your Values
28. Secret of Healing Conversations: Ethical Practices in Counselling and Therapy
29. Creative Kindness: Crafting a Life of Compassion and Creativity
30. The Power of Appreciation: How Gratitude Can Transform Your Relationships
31. Bhagavad-Gita: Messages
32. Science of Art: The New Frontier of Fashion Modernism
33. Vivekananda's Virtues: A Blueprint for Modern Living
34. Empower Her: Navigating the Path to Women's Entrepreneurship
35. The Boundless Classroom: Innovations in Global Education
36. The Language of Leadership: Communicating with Authenticity and Impact
37. The Warrior's Mantra: Deciphering the Hanuman Chalisa
38. Echoes of Empathy: Transformative Stories of Social Service
39. Artful Living: Cultivating Creativity in Your Daily Routine
40. Finding Your Why: Discovering Your Passions and Charting Your Course
41. The Role of Social Media in Shaping Self-Esteem and Interpersonal Relationships among Adolescents

ƊƊƊ

Contact

Dr. Minakshi Bansal
Social Activist
Ahmedabad, Gujarat, Bharat
minakshiindiag20@yahoo.com

❦❦❦

|| LOKAHA SAMASTHAHA SUKHINO BHAVANTU ||

● 131 ●